My Mom is a Superhero

Dr. Federica Robinson-Bryant

My Mom is a Superhero

Published by Denotion Research Group
www.DenotionResearch.com

Cover & Illustrations by Tullip Studio

ISBN:
978-1-958634-37-0 (2nd edition)
978-1-958634-04-2 (1st edition)
978-1-958634-05-9 (eBook)

Printed in United States
2nd Edition

Dedication

This book is dedicated to my first and greatest mission:
Amiyah, Amani, Ahmari & Ahkeem.
May you forever be grounded in your purpose
and bravely move forward.

Of all the wonders I have known,
I have discovered the best one yet.
My mom is a superhero!
And here's why I'm telling you that!

She awakes early every morning,
to check the many boxes on her list.
Mom always confirms that we have what we need,
before giving each cereal-dusted cheek a kiss.

Mom takes the scenic routes to our schools, unloading us one-by-one. She points out different structures and fun facts, to show that there's always more to see and learn.

My mom is a superhero,
in the form of a motherhood guru!

Mom heads to her job as an engineer-
A systems engineer as a matter of fact.

She's an engineer that helps to realize systems,
applying ideas and tools from the many fields that intersect.

One day she's defining how machines work.
The next, she's investigating energy's flow.
She can even reverse engineer my favorite toys,
and has modernized older systems from long ago.

My mom is a superhero,
in the form of an engineering guru!

My mom is a superhero,
in the form of a systems guru.

Vocabulary

Advocate	Flow
Anticipate	Form
Balance	Function
Complex	Intersect
Conclusion	Investigate
Constraint	Junction
Define	Machine
Discover	Modernize
Energy	Multi-faceted
Engineer	Navigate
Fact	Need
Field	Peer
Fit	Process

Vocabulary

Project

Purpose

Realize

Reasonable

Requirement

Reverse Engineer

Structure

System

Systems Approach

Systems Engineering

Tool